WITH APPROVAL:

A theological exploration of blessing

WITH GOD'S APPROVAL?

A theological exploration of blessing same-sex couples, in dialogue with Walter Moberly and Isabelle Hamley

This paper was written as a contribution to the discussions in the Church of England concerning the *Prayers of Love and Faith* proposals from the House of Bishops.

© Martin Davie 2023

Published by Dictum Press, Oxford, UK

www.dictumpress.com

ISBN 978-1-915934-19-2

First published July 2023

Designed by Chris Gander

CONTENTS

WITH GOD'S APPROVAL?

A theological exploration of blessing same-sex couples, in dialogue with Walter Moberly and Isabelle Hamley

In February 2023 the House of Bishops published a set of liturgical resources entitled *Prayers of Love and Faith* as part of their response to the Church of England's *Living in Love and Faith* process. The Pastoral Introduction states that they:

> .... are commended by the House of Bishops as resources in praying with and for two people who love one another and who wish to give thanks for and mark that love in faith before God. To celebrate in God's presence the commitment two people have made to each other is an occasion for rejoicing. The texts are offered to express thanksgiving and hope, with prayer that those who are dedicating their life together to God may grow in faith, love and service as God's blessing rests upon them.[1]

Among those for whom the resources are intended are same-sex couples, including those who have 'registered a civil partnership, or entered into a civil marriage'[2] and no distinction is made with regard to whether the relationships involved are sexually active or sexually abstinent.

---

1. The House of Bishops, *Prayers of Love and Faith* (London: CHP 2023), p2

The overarching theological issue raised by these new resources is whether it is theologically possible to hold that God's blessing can rest upon sexually-active same-sex relationships and same-sex marriages, and thus, whether it is legitimate for the Church of England to authorise such prayers.

The purpose of my paper is to address that issue. The paper is in three parts.

Part I gives an introduction to two papers on blessing by Professor Walter Moberly[3] and Isabelle Hamley,[4] which were produced as part of the *Living in Love and Faith* process and which contributed to the discussions among the bishops that led to *Prayers of Love and Faith*.

Part II brings a critical examination of each. Here I argue that neither of these papers provides a persuasive argument for thinking that God's blessing can rest upon sexually-active same-sex relationships.

Part III explores what we learn about blessing from the Bible. I argue that the Bible contains a clear pattern for God's blessing of his human creatures. According to this pattern, receiving God's blessing involves living in trusting obedience to God's kingly

---

2. The House of Bishops, *Living in Love and Faith – A response from the Bishops of the Church of England about identity, sexuality, relationships and marriage* (London: CHP, 2023), p6

3. The Revd Professor Walter Moberly, a biblical scholar, is Emeritus Professor in the Department of Theology and Religion the University of Durham.

4. The Revd Prebendary Dr Isabelle Hamley is Theological Adviser to the House of Bishops of the Church of England, and Secretary for Theology and Ecumenical Relations. She is a visiting fellow at King's College London.

rule. Part of that obedience is observing God's decision that (i) marriage be between a man and a woman; (ii) sexual activity be confined to this context, and (iii) same-sex sexual relationships are off limits for God's people.

It follows that to institute prayers for the blessing of same-sex sexual relationships and same-sex marriages as proposed in *Prayers of Love and Faith* would be to reject the sovereignty and consistency of God, since it would involve failing to accept God's sovereign decision concerning what he will bless, and deciding that God's rejection of same-sex sexual activity no longer applies.

PART I

An introduction to the papers by
Walter Moberly and Isabelle Hamley

I shall first summarise the papers by Moberly and Hamley, then critically examine the strengths and weaknesses of their arguments.

1. Walter Moberly *Blessing*

Professor Walter Moberly's paper *Blessing* (which can be found online in the library section of the *Living in Love and Faith* site) begins by noting that the 2003 Doctrine Commission report *Being Human* argued that Anglicanism should be seen as 'a wisdom tradition for the twenty-first century.'[5]

He further notes that according to this report:

> Wisdom is not primarily about accepting certain conclusions. It is about the habits of individuals and communities. These habits of mind, heart, imagination and will can help us, in the ever-changing circumstances of our lives, to find a wisdom that is in line with the purposes of God.[6]

Moberly then goes on to say that at the heart of wisdom lies the interpretation of Scripture and then suggests that since the pursuit of Scripturally-based

5. Walter Moberly, *Blessing*, p1 quoting The Doctrine Commission, *Being Human* (London: CHP, 2003), p7
6. Moberly, p1 quoting *Being Human*, p12

wisdom is 'basic to LLF' it follows that we need to ask how it might apply to 'the specifics of current concerns with issues of sex and sexuality.'[7]

At the start of his answer to this question, Moberly declares that our understanding of wisdom in regard to these issues may be changing:

> The extensive testimony, literature and practice of gay, lesbian and bisexual Christians in recent years creates a *prima facie* case for some change in public Christian practice. To be sure, some Christians are unpersuaded that any change is appropriate, or, if there is to be change, what form it might best take. But there has already been change in the acceptance of civil partnerships: celibate for ordinands and clergy but not necessarily celibate for lay people. Moreover, it is hard even for those traditionally inclined, if they genuinely engage with both the people and the literature, to come away unmoved and unrecognizing that in significant respects things have changed from how they were fifty years ago. Faithful committed Christians make the case for same-sex relationships in a way that used not to happen. To recognize this is not necessarily to agree. But it is to recognize that what counts as Christian wisdom may in some ways be changing.[8]

He further adds that Christians need to recognise that they have a limited understanding of what is happening today and that therefore any conclusions they reach must be viewed as provisional:

7. Moberly, p1
8. Moberly, pp1-2

.... our quest for a wisdom that is rooted in the interpretation of Scripture not only requires fidelity to the given content of Christian faith. It also requires creativity in grasping what that content might mean in a changed and changing world. And a good starting point is an honest recognition of our limited understanding of what is currently going on. This means that there must be a greater-than-usual provisionality about any proposals we come up with. We must decide what makes best sense for us here and now, in a way that does not prejudge what will necessarily be the case in other places and in the future.[9]

Moving on to look at what Scripture might offer us in the development of this kind of provisional wisdom, Moberly next states that the study of the biblical passages relating to same-sex issues undertaken by LLF shows that they do not provide a sufficient guide for the current practice of the Church of England. In his words:

Elsewhere in LLF we have a detailed study of those biblical passages which handle same-sex issues. This concludes that there is no clear fit or match between that of which the biblical writers disapprove and that which advocates for faithful and stable same-sex partnerships propose. The biblical texts of disapproval remain on the table, as it were, as part of Scripture; yet the result of careful study is that it is unsafe to suppose that these passages in themselves are a sufficient guide to what the CoE should, or should not, do today.[10]

This being the case, writes Moberly, we need to look elsewhere in Scripture for 'resources for thinking freshly about our overall stance and approach.'[11] In his view what the Bible says about blessing provides us with such a resource:

> Blessing is a core concept and practice in both Old and New Testament, and has a long and rich history in the life of the Church. The biblical understanding of blessing may offer us a fruitful way ahead.[12]

Moberly then goes on to cite and comment on a series of instances of blessing found in the Bible.

First, he cites God's blessing of animate life and human beings in Genesis 1:22 and 28, which express 'God's intrinsic goodwill towards the created order, the divine desire for its flourishing.'[13]

Secondly, he cites God's blessing of the Sabbath in Genesis 2:1-3, which shows 'part of the blessing of animate life relates to life having a particular context which will contribute to the realization of that blessing.'[14]

Thirdly, he cites God's blessing of Abraham and his descendants in Genesis 12:1-3 to be both a model of blessing and a 'means of conveying blessing to

---

10. Moberly, p2
11. Moberly, p2
12. Moberly, p2
13. Moberly, p3
14. Moberly, p3

other people on earth' (which is how this blessing is understood by Paul in Galatians 3:6-8).[15]

Fourthly, he cites God's blessing of Ishmael in Genesis 17:20 in which 'God extends blessing even to the one whose descendants will create problems.'[16]

Fifthly, he cites the Aaronic blessing to be pronounced over the whole people of Israel (Numbers 6:22-27), a passage which he says 'gives the fullest explicit articulation of the meaning and implications of blessing' in terms of God keeping, being gracious to, giving peace to, and shining upon (ie smiling upon) his people.[17]

Sixthly, he cites the injunctions for Christians to bless those who 'persecute, curse and abuse them' (Romans 12:14, Luke 6:28), injunctions which 'envisage Christians actively and prayerfully engaging with God, that what is good for these people should come to them from God (without prescribing what form that should take).'[18]

Finally, he notes what he sees as the tension in Scripture between blessing as unconditional, and as conditional upon obedience:

There is an important and constructive tension in the portrayal of blessing as a whole in the Bible. On the one hand, it represents the sovereign and gracious initiative of God towards creation. On the other hand, there are passages which speak of blessing being

---

15. Moberly, p3
16. Moberly, p3
17. Moberly, p4
18. Moberly, p4

received in the covenantal context of human obedience to God (Deuteronomy 28:1-14). This tension between 'God sovereignly blesses' and 'God blesses those who are obedient' is not something to be resolved, but articulates some of the dimensions of love, where love is both unconditionally given and love only thrives when there is mutuality and responsiveness. The tension between grace freely given, and the need for trusting and obedient responsiveness in relation to it, runs through Scripture as a whole.[19]

According to Moberly, the biblical material he has surveyed:

.... offers a possible outlook and pattern for the church today. In general terms, Christians who trust and hope in God's good purposes for creation can appropriately reflect that in their dealings with each other and with society generally in seeking to affirm God's blessing on those around them. Discernment of problems and warning against folly remain part of the Christian vocation, but not at the cost of muting God's fundamental desire to bless.[20]

As he sees it, the best way to articulate this in relation to 'gay, lesbian and bisexual Christians' is through a formal blessing of same-sex covenant partnerships with no expectation of celibacy.[21] In his view, this would be preferable to same-sex marriage because this:

... arguably 'normalizes' same-sex relationships too quickly, without asking whether there is any particular gift, or indeed blessing, that same-sex couples, as same-sex couples, might contribute to church and world.[22]

2. Isabelle Hamley *Blessing*

Dr Isabelle Hamley's paper, also found in the LLF library is, too, called *Blessing*.

As Hamley explains at the beginning of her paper, its purpose is to explore:

> .... what we mean by 'blessing' in a Christian context, and how the notion of blessing can be brought to bear on appropriate forms of prayer which may be offered to same-sex couples.

> The first two sections are explicitly theological, and explore briefly the meaning and nature of blessing. The next section looks more specifically at the symbolism of blessing in relation to marriage and relationships, and the final section considers possible options for prayers.

> This is a paper designed to provoke thinking and conversation, and to explore the subject from a variety of angles.[23]

Hamley starts by reviewing the biblical material relating to blessing, building on the section in Moberly's paper, and quoting much of it verbatim.

---

19. Moberly, p4
20. Moberly, p5
21. Moberly, p5
22. Moberly, p5
23. Hamley, p1

However, she adds three things to what Moberly writes.

First, she comments on blessing in the Psalms and the Old Testament wisdom literature as follows:

> The Psalms and wisdom corpus draw on a slightly different aspect of 'blessing'. Blessing is a consequence, an outcome, of a life of pursuing holiness and righteousness. The wisdom Psalms repeatedly locate blessing in the Torah and following the ways of the Lord. It is not that following the ways of God is needed in order to gain blessing; but rather that blessing is fully realised and augmented when living a godly life. The Psalms also contain a number of references to people blessing God, suggesting an iterative relationship of blessing as people grow into the life of faith, which enables them to be 'blessed' and 'blesses' God in return.[24]

Secondly, Hamley notes that the same Hebrew word is used for 'bless' and 'curse' in the Book of Job:

> The book of Job problematises the word 'bless' by using one word only to speak of both blessing and curse (a common scribal device); as such, the book questions whether human beings are able to recognise and name what a true 'blessing' looks like, and suggests that they often confuse material gains and an easy life with a blessed life. This tension is picked up in other texts, and, in the New Testament, in the Sermon on the Mount and the Beatitudes.[25]

24. Hamley, p2

Thirdly, Hamley adds to Moberly's discussion of the tension between the unconditional nature of God's blessing and the need for an obedient response by declaring:

> This tension sets blessing as a form of calling: recognising that all things belong to God and come from God, but also that everything is being drawn into God's transforming grace. Blessing both affirms God's initial creative intent and orients us into God's work of redemption and re-creation.[26]

Hamley summarises what she thinks we can learn from blessing about Scripture in nine bullet points:

- It represents more than a discrete act, and symbolises a posture towards the world
- It is rooted in the divine desire for the whole of creation to flourish
- It is people that are blessed primarily (together with other animate life), even when their actions might cause concern; in this way, God's blessing reflects an intention to see, and enable the other to, flourish
- The conditions within which human beings may flourish can also be blessed, such as the Sabbath
- Flourishing is given shape and fullness in conjunction with godly virtues – peace, grace, orientation towards the good of the 'other'
- There is a link between blessing and fruitfulness, though this is not tied solely to procreation

25. Hamley, p2
26. Hamley, p2

- There is an implied cascade of blessing where a blessed individual in turn shares blessings with others
- Human beings are not terribly good at defining what constitutes 'blessing'
- There is an ongoing dialectical relationship between blessing and holiness, reflected in practical tensions in the Church between celebrating-without-purifying and purifying-without-celebrating, as Andrew Davison puts it.[27]

Hamley then goes on to consider what it signifies or expresses when Christians today engage in acts of blessing. Her answer is that:

> At its most basic ... the action of blessing represents a reflection of God's intent that another person flourish, and a prayer for them to come into God's life in all its fulness, as defined by God (and therefore 'holy'). As such, blessings relate both to God's creation and to human vocation. One short-hand for blessing might be 'invoking God's power for the good of that which is blessed'. Associated with the direct blessing of people, there may be an acknowledgement that certain conditions or ways of life may be such 'good' that they may in themselves be a blessing or nurture flourishing and blessing – and it is this understanding that shapes the Marriage Service.[28]

Building on this understanding of what acts of blessing mean, Hamley further writes that:

---

27. Hamley, p3
28. Hamley, p5

The marriage service therefore blesses an individual couple, and affirms marriage as a 'good' within which blessing is more likely to be experienced in its fullness. This understanding of marriage does not preclude the possibility of other relationships being good, or warranting some form of blessing, but it does set aside marriage as a distinctive form of life.[29]

As Hamley sees it, what this means is that the conversation within the Church about the possibility of same-sex marriages needs to have two elements:

Part of the conversation on whether to move towards either same-sex marriages or same-sex blessings needs to address what the 'goods' of a relationship are; whether the goods of a same-sex relationship are identical to those of marriage, or whether they have sufficient resemblance to those of marriage to be brought together; how these goods are acknowledged and affirmed, and how God's intention to bless can be extended generously and in keeping with the dual orientation of creation and vocation.

The conversation also needs to recognise that to bless a relationship is an act that shapes the social imagination, and puts those who are blessed into a new type of relationship not just towards one another, but towards the collective imagination. Conversely, choosing what not to bless is also a defining act of social imagination, and sets people into specific relationship to communities

---

29. Hamley, p6

and their understanding of ethics, faith and holiness. When officially choosing either to bless or refuse to bless, the Church sends a powerful signal about acceptability, inclusion and ethics. Liturgy and practice shape doctrine, and any form of public prayer is also a de facto form of teaching.[30]

Hamley next considers the issues of whether same-sex blessings could be offered instead of marriage and whether this would constitute a change in the Church's doctrine.

On the first of these issues, she declares:

> The idea that it may be possible to offer 'blessing' as an option other than Holy Matrimony could be based on an understanding of blessing as the blessing of people, and prayer for growth in holiness. A prayer of blessing specifically over the relationship would imply a judgement that this relationship is in keeping with what we understand of God's divine purposes, at which point one may either declare that this could be just as easily reflected through a marriage ceremony; conversely, it is possible to argue that while the relationship is good in being faithful, stable and permanent, and may be fruitful in hospitality and generosity towards others, it is nevertheless different from Holy Matrimony, (in what specific ways would need to be clearly stated), and needs to be recognised as such and blessed in its difference.[31]

---

31. Hamley, p7

As Hamley sees it, this kind of blessing could take a variety of forms.

First, there could be the 'blessing of a distinctive covenanted way of life.' This form of blessing:

> .... could affirm the goods of same-sex relationships as a distinctive way of life within which blessing is to be found, in the same way as marriage is affirmed in the marriage service. This would set up forms of same-sex relationships as 'a way of life made holy by God', yet position them as different from marriage.[32]

Hamley concedes that:

> This could imply a change in teaching if the way of life that is recognised is one that includes sexual intimacy (given the traditional teaching that marriage is the only place where sexuality is rightly expressed).[33]

However, she also argues that:

> ... the extent to which the canons state that marriage is the only appropriate place for sexual intimacy is contested. The relevant canon is B30. This speaks strongly of (sexual) exclusiveness and fidelity within marriage, ie for those who are married, but does not seem itself to point to marriage as the only place where sexuality is rightly expressed for all people. It is true that B30 does point to the teaching of the Book of Common Prayer, and the BCP preface to the marriage service speaks of marriage being given 'to avoid fornication' for

---

32. Hamley, p7
33. Hamley, p7

those who 'have not the gift of continency'. However, there is no mention of any of this in the Common Worship marriage preface. That does not mean that this teaching is not still in the background, but it is no longer foregrounded in the same way, which may imply that in the contemporary Church's view it is of less significance than the core doctrine of marriage as an 'exclusive lifelong faithful mutual commitment of man and woman'.[34]

Secondly, there could be the blessing of celibate 'covenanted friendships'. This kind of blessing, writes Hamley, would 'specifically rule out sexual activity as a part of the relationship' and for this reason it could be instituted 'without any contradiction with current doctrine.'[35] She further notes that there is '... no obvious reason why this type of blessing service should be reserved to same-sex couples, or indeed to 'couples' since it is primarily about friendship.'[36]

Thirdly, there could be the blessing of an existing same-sex civil marriage. Hamley makes two points about this option.

(i) in her view this service would 'be offered mostly by churches not offering to perform same-sex marriages' as an act of pastoral hospitality. If this were the case:

... it would need to be made clear why a church is willing to bless a same-sex civil marriage but

---

34. Hamley, p7
35. Hamley, p8
36. Hamley, p8

not willing to marry same-sex couples. So, for example, it might be that a distinction is being drawn between the goods of a same-sex civil marriage (which are being blessed) and the goods of Holy Matrimony. If so, it would need to be made clear in what ways this might or might not apply to opposite-sex couples seeking a blessing following a civil marriage.[37]

(ii) there would also be the problem that:

.... this position runs the risk of being perceived as confusing (and perhaps disingenuous) in simultaneously affirming and rejecting same-sex marriage. As such, while this option could be seen as a 'compromise' or as indicating a direction of travel towards same-sex marriage, the pastoral and theological coherence of the option seems difficult to maintain.[38]

Finally, Hamley notes two further options:

1. To use the existing service of Prayer and Dedication after a Civil Marriage for those who have entered into a civil same-sex marriage 'as an alternative either to SSM in church, or to a service of blessing.'

In her view, questions arise from this proposal. The current service draws a strong parallel with Holy Matrimony, and therefore it is not entirely clear why this would be a softer alternative to blessing or SSM.

37. Hamley, p8
38. Hamley, p8

- Would same-sex couples be offered the same liturgy as opposite-sex couples? If so, how do we make sense of the strength of association between civil marriage and Holy Matrimony?
- Would same-sex couples be offered a *different* liturgy? If so, would this liturgy drive a stronger wedge between civil and church marriage, and what would the effect be on opposite-sex couples? And would such an option be regarded as very much second-rate?
- How does this service offer a full alternative to 'blessing', and how would the difference be conceptualised and explained? (In practice, couples already think of this as a blessing of their marriage, even if the service is not entitled 'blessing').[39]

2. To use the outline service of 'Thanksgiving for marriage' from the *Common Worship* Pastoral Services. However, the wording of this service ties it closely to Holy Matrimony and therefore also raises problems.
    According to Hamley:

    Both of these services relate back to the words, forms and theology of Holy Matrimony; adapting them for use after a same-sex civil marriage therefore implies stretching, expanding or changing the doctrine of marriage as expressed through the canons and BCP, and agreeing an alternative to the texts to reflect these

---

39. Hamley, p10

changes. With both options, the question remains as to why a church that refuses to perform same-sex marriages would nevertheless dedicate or bless civil marriages – unless it decided to drive a much clearer wedge between civil marriage and Holy Matrimony.[40]

40. Hamley, p11

PART II

A critical examination of the papers by Moberly and Hamley
(Both entitled *Blessing*)

1. An examination of *Blessing* by Moberly

Moberly is correct to say that the Church of England needs to think about how to respond with wisdom to 'current issues of sex and sexuality.' In the Christian tradition, wisdom is understanding how practically to apply our knowledge of God in the specific situations we encounter, both as individuals and collectively as the Church of Christ.

He is also correct to say that the interpretation of Scripture lies at the heart of wisdom. As Scripture is our primary resource for knowing God and his will for our lives, wisdom necessarily involves interpreting Scripture rightly so we can then apply its teaching correctly.

Unfortunately, the rest of what Moberly says does not help us with our task of determining how the Church of England should respond with wisdom to current issues regarding sex and sexuality in the light of a right interpretation of Scripture. This is for the following reasons:

First, he does not give any evidence to support his claim that 'extensive testimony, literature and practice of gay, lesbian and bisexual Christians in recent years creates a *prima facie* case for some change in public Christian practice.' For this claim to be plausible, he would need to show that the testimony, literature and practice to which he refers gives us knowledge of God's will regarding human sexuality that we either did not possess, or had forgotten, and that that points us to the need to change the Church's existing practice. However, he does not do this.

The two pieces of evidence he gives in support of his argument are that there has been 'a change in the acceptance of Civil Partnerships' and that 'faithful committed Christians make the case for same-sex relationships in a way that used not to happen.'

In regard to Civil Partnerships, he fails to explain what he means by the 'acceptance 'of Civil Partnerships and fails to note that the position of the Church of England is that it is not right for those in same-sex Civil Partnerships to be in a sexually-active same-sex relationships or for Civil Partnerships to be blessed in Church. These two points are made, for example, in the pastoral guidance on Civil Partnerships issued by the House of Bishops in 2005. This declares:

.... the Church of England teaches that 'sexual intercourse, as an expression of faithful intimacy, properly belongs within marriage exclusively' (Marriage: a teaching document of the House of Bishops, 1999). Sexual relationships outside marriage, whether heterosexual or between people of the same sex, are regarded as falling short of God's purposes for human beings.[41]

---

41. The House of Bishops, 'Civil Partnerships: A pastoral statement from the House of Bishops of the Church of England,' 2005, p1

and further states that 'it would not be right to produce an authorised public liturgy in connection with the registering of civil partnerships' and 'clergy of the Church of England should not provide services of blessing for those who register a civil partnership.'[42]

Both of these points were reiterated by the House of Bishops in their 2019 Pastoral Guidance following the introduction of Civil Partnerships between people of the opposite sex, and the position of the Church of England has not been revised since. So what acceptance is Moberly talking about?

In regard to his second claim, it is simply not true that committed Christians 'make the case for same-sex relationships in a way that used not to happen.' If you track the current debate about how Christians should respond to same-sex relationships back to its origin in the 1960s, you will find that the arguments put forward for the Christian acceptance of same-sex relationships have remained the same, the observed quality of such relationships, the unloving nature of refusing to allow gay, lesbian and bisexual people to be in a sexual relationship, and the possibility of interpreting Scripture in a gay affirming fashion.[43] Over the past sixty years these arguments have not led the Church of England to change its teaching and practice with regard to same-sex relationships. What Moberly does not explain is why they should do so now.

---

42. Op cit p4
43. For the evidence for this point see Chapter 2 of Richard Lovelace, *Homosexuality and the Church* (London: Lamp Press 1979)

Secondly, he does not explain why our 'limited understanding of what is currently going on' means that 'there must be a greater-than-usual provisionality about any proposals we come up with.' It is of course true that in this life Christians have a limited degree of understanding. In Paul's words 'we see in a mirror dimly' and 'know in part' (1 Corinthians 13:12).

However, this truth has not stopped Christians from New Testament times onwards holding that they can and should make clear statements about the limits of acceptable sexual conduct. They have held that they have enough knowledge to judge that such statements are both possible and necessary. What Moberly does not tell us is why this is no longer the case. Why is everything suddenly more uncertain today? It cannot be because people now want to have sex outside heterosexual marriage (including gay and lesbian sex) since this has been the case throughout the history of the Church. So what does he think has changed?

Thirdly, Moberly is mistaken when he declares that the *Living in Love and Faith* material has shown that there is 'no clear fit or match between that of which the biblical writers disapprove and that which advocates for faithful and stable same-sex partnerships propose' and that therefore it is 'unsafe to suppose that these passages in themselves are a sufficient guide to what the CoE should, or should not, do today.'

This claim is problematic for two reasons.

(a) The LLF material itself does not make this claim.
What LLF actually says at the end of its review
of some of the key texts that have been seen
as forbidding same-sex sexual activity (Genesis
19, Leviticus 18:22 and 20:13, Romans 1:26-27, 1
Corinthians 6:9-11, and 1 Timothy 8:11) is:

> Until relatively recently they were universally and
> uncontroversially read as consistently rejecting all same-
> sex sexual behaviour. We have seen, however, that some
> now question this and interpret them as more narrowly
> focused, so leaving open the possibility of approving
> faithful, committed same- sex relationships.[44]

It is an unjustifiable move on Moberly's part to
construe 'some now question' as meaning 'we now
know.' The two are not the same.

(b) Even the more tentative statement that LLF
actually makes needs qualification in order to
reflect the current state of biblical scholarship
more accurately. Chapter 13 of LLF is correct to
note that some pro-gay writers have questioned
whether the biblical texts it reviews do rule out
same-sex relationships today. What it fails to
note, however, is that the interpretation of these
texts offered by pro-gay writers referred to in
that chapter, has been refuted time and again

---

44. The Church of England, *Living in Love and Faith* (London: CHP, 2020),
p294

by conservative scholars[45] to the extent that even a number of pro-gay scholars have now ceased to doubt that the texts mean what they have always been understood to mean. Thus, the American biblical scholars Walter Wink and Luke Johnson (both of whom are supportive of same-sex relationships) have written 'Where the Bible mentions homosexual behaviour at all, it clearly condemns it' and that 'we do, in fact, reject the straightforward commands of Scripture, and appeal instead to another authority when we declare that same-sex unions can be holy and good.'[46]

If Moberly wants to substantiate the claim he makes about the biblical material, he has to do the heavy lifting of showing that the work of all the scholars I have just cited is wrong. He does no such thing.

Fourthly, there are two problems with Moberly's survey of the biblical material regarding blessing.

---

45. See, for example, Michael Brown, *Can you be Gay and Christian?* (Lake Mary: Front line, 2014); Richard Davidson, *Flame of Yahweh – Sexuality in the Old Testament* (Peabody: Hendrickson, 2007), Chapter 4; Martin Davie, *Studies in the Bible and same-sex relationships since 2003* (Malton: Gilead Books 2013); Kevin De Young, *What does the Bible really teach about homosexuality?* (Nottingham: Inter-Varsity Press, 2015); Robert Gagnon, *The Bible and Homosexual Practice* (Nashville: Abingdon Press, 2001); William Loader, *The New Testament on Sexuality* (Grand Rapids: Eerdmans, 2012); Ian Paul, *Same-sex Unions – The Key Biblical Texts* (Cambridge: Grove Books, 2014); and Donald Wold, *Out of Order* (Grand Rapids: Baker Books, 1998).
46. Walter Wink, *Homosexuality and the Bible* (New York: Fellowship Bookstore, 1996) and Luke Timothy Johnson https://www.commonwealmagazine.org/homosexuality-church-1 accessed 1 May 2023

(i) some of what he says about this material is
     misleading for the following reasons:

It is not the case that the point being made in
Genesis 17:20 is that 'God extends blessing even to
the one whose descendants will create problems.'
In context the point of this verse is to differentiate
between the blessings bestowed upon Ishmael and
upon Isaac. As John Calvin puts it, in this verse God:

> ...more clearly discriminates between the two sons of
> Abraham. For in promising to the one wealth, dignity and
> other things pertaining to the present life, he proves
> him to be a son according to the flesh. But he makes a
> special covenant with Isaac, which rises above this world
> and this frail life: not for the sake of cutting Ishmael
> off from the hope of eternal life, but in order to teach
> him that salvation is to be sought from the race of Isaac
> where it really dwells.[47]

It follows that Genesis 17:20 cannot rightly be used
as a justification for blessing same-sex couples even
if their behaviour is ethically problematic. To say this
is to distort the point the text is making.

What this text does contribute to the debate is the
truth that God sets limits to the context in which the
blessing of eternal life will be received. In the Bible
that blessing has to be received through being part
of the people of God descended from Abraham and
Isaac, and living in obedience to God in that context.
The question which this then raises is whether being

---

47. John Calvin, *Genesis* (Edinburgh: Banner of Truth, 1984), p462

in a same-sex sexual relationship is consistent with such obedience.

The injunctions to Christians to bless those who persecute, curse and abuse them do not specifically lay down the precise form that God's blessing should be expected to take. However, the consistency of God's actions means that whatever specific form such blessing takes, it will not be contrary to the shape of the blessing generally promised by God in Scripture, namely a right relationship with God in this world, leading to an eternity spent enjoying God's presence in the world to come. This being the case, we cannot pray that God will bless those in a same-sex sexual relationship if it is the case (as the Church has traditionally held) that being in a same-sex sexual relationship prevents people from enjoying a right relationship with God in this world and spending eternity with him in the life to come.

(ii) It is not the case that there is in Scripture a 'tension between grace freely given, and the need for trusting and obedient responsiveness.' That is because free grace and trusting and obedient responsiveness are not two different things that stand over and against each other. God's grace is free in the sense that he is under no external compulsion to bestow it, but in Scripture the character of the grace that God bestows is the ability to respond to God in a life of trusting obedience.

We can see this for example in Ephesians 2:8-10 where Paul writes:

For by grace you have been saved by faith; and this is not your own doing, it is the gift of God – not because of works, lest any man should boast. For we are his workmanship, created in Christ Jesus for good works, which God prepared beforehand, that we should walk in them.

Here everything described is a matter of grace, and central to that grace is the fact that God makes Christians into people who live lives characterised by obedience to God, manifesting itself in the performance of 'good works,' ie actions that are in accordance with the will of God. To receive grace is to receive this power to obey and to act accordingly. In relation to same-sex sexual relationships the question this raises is whether or not such relationships are actions which manifest the obedience-creating grace of God.

Fifthly, Moberly makes an unjustified link between God's 'desire to bless' and the blessing of same-sex sexual relationships (which Moberly thinks should take the form of the blessing of same-sex covenanted partnerships). It is clearly true that God does have a 'desire to bless,' or else no blessing would ever take place. However, it is an unjustifiable leap to say God desires to bless, and therefore this means that it is right for the Church to bless same-sex sexual relationships.

What we have to ask is whether such relationships are compatible with enjoying a right relationship with God in this world, leading to an eternity spent enjoying God's presence in the world to come. Only if we can answer 'yes' to this question can we say that they can be the objects of God's blessing and therefore something on which the Church can pray that God's blessing will rest.

Moberly does not show that this is the case.

2. An examination of *Blessing* by Hamley

If we move on to the paper by Hamley, we find that this, too, is problematic.

First, Hamley is right to say that, in the Psalms and wisdom literature, blessing involves walking in the ways of the Lord as laid out in the Torah. We can see this, for example, in Psalm 1:

Blessed is the man
who walks not in the counsel of the wicked,
nor stands in the way of sinners,
nor sits in the seat of scoffers;
but his delight is in the law of the Lord,
and on his law he meditates day and night.
He is like a tree
planted by streams of water,
that yields its fruit in its season,
and its leaf does not wither.
In all that he does, he prospers. (Psalm 1:1-3)

However this understanding of what blessing involves is not unique to the Psalms and the Wisdom literature. It is the consistent teaching of the Bible as whole, the New Testament as well as the Old (see Matthew 5:17-19; Romans 3:31, 8:3-4). Blessing is not, as Hamley suggests, 'fully realised and augmented when living a godly life.' This suggests that God's blessing is somehow increased ('augmented') when we lead a godly life. As we have seen, living a godly life is not something additional to being blessed. God fully blesses us; our living a godly life is not an augmentation of this blessing but simply living it out. We can block our enjoyment of God's blessing by our disobedience. What we cannot do is increase God's blessing by our obedience.

Secondly, Hamley misrepresents the significance of the use of Hebrew verb *barak* (normally meaning 'bless') to mean 'curse' in Job 1:5, 1:11, 2:5, 2:9. There is nothing in these verses to suggest that the 'bless' and 'curse' carry the same meaning or that what these verses are meant to teach us is the difficulty human beings have in being 'able to recognise and name what a true "blessing" looks like.' These verses are not concerned with the different kinds of blessing that human beings receive from God but with the action of human beings in potentially cursing God rather than blessing him.

Scholars offer a variety of explanations for this use of *barak*, but the most plausible is that it is a euphemism designed to avoid using the word curse in relation to God, or that *barak* can mean 'bid farewell to' and by extension 'reject', and so what is being envisaged is Job or his sons rejecting God.

Thirdly, like Moberly, Hamley, too, writes about the 'tension' between blessing and obedience, an idea which is problematic for the reasons previously noted. She also declares that the concept of blessing involves: 'recognising that all things belong to God and come from God, but also that everything is being drawn into God's transforming grace.' The first half of this statement is true but the second ignores the fact that grace can be, and is, resisted. God has created creatures (angels and humans) who can and do say 'no' to him, and resist his good purposes.

Fourthly, Hamley declares that people can be blessed 'even when their actions might cause concern.' As we have seen, this is not what Genesis 17:20 is about, and furthermore it needs to be recognised that while God does bless those whose actions cause concern (as when God blesses Paul the persecutor) this does not mean that ungodly actions are ever blessed. There is nothing in Scripture to suggest that God ever blesses sin.

Fifthly, when Hamley writes that human beings 'are not terribly good at defining what constitutes "blessing"' this is true, but what she does not then go on to say is that Scriptures come to our aid at this point by telling us what blessing involves. To use a famous image from Calvin, 'Scripture functions like a pair of spectacles correcting our blurred vision in this regard.'[48]

Sixthly, it is not the case, as Hamley argues, that there is 'an ongoing dialectical relationship between blessing and holiness.' As we have noted, the relationship between the two is not 'dialectical' in

---

48. See John Calvin, *Institutes*, Book 1:6:1

the sense that blessing and holiness are two things which stand over against each other. When someone or something is 'blessed' this means that they are enabled to live a holy life in obedience to God ('You shall be holy, for I the Lord your God am holy' (Leviticus 19:2, 1 Peter 1:15-16) or (in the case of an object) set apart for God's service, and in this sense rendered sacred or 'holy.' Blessing and holiness thus go together.

Seventhly, Hamley's definition of what it means for humans to engage in blessing others is helpful: 'the action of blessing represents a reflection of God's intent that another person flourish, and a prayer for them to come into God's life in all its fulness, as defined by God (and therefore 'holy').'

However, she does not consider the question of whether same-sex sexual relationships, including same-sex marriages, are ways of life that are capable of being holy in the sense of being part of 'God's life in all its fulness' as defined by him.

As Hamley must be aware, the view that the Christian Church has taken throughout its history, and the view that the majority of the Church around the world still holds today, is that the answer to this question is 'no.' This is because same-sex sexual activity has been (and is) seen as something which Scripture describes as sinful, and therefore a relationship involving such activity cannot be holy and, as such, part of God's life in all its fulness. In addition, entering into a same-sex marriage is also seen as sinful because it involves making a decision about what marriage can be that goes against God's creation of marriage as a relationship between two people of the opposite sex.

The second half of Hamley's paper discusses the pros and cons of the various forms which the blessing of same-sex relationships in the Church of England could take, but unless she can show that the Church has been (and is) wrong in its assessment of same-sex sexual relationships as sinful, this whole discussion (with the exception of the discussion of the blessing of celibate friendships) is illegitimate, since it is a discussion of how to perform the impossible task of blessing sin. It would be like holding a discussion of the pros and cons of different forms of the blessing of adultery or theft.

Eighthly, Hamley's account of teaching of Canon B.30 is misleading. When she writes that this Canon 'does not seem itself to point to marriage as the only place where sexuality is rightly expressed for all people' she has failed to understand what the Canon means when it lists the second purpose of marriage as 'the hallowing and right direction of the natural instincts and affections.'

The words 'for the hallowing and right direction of the natural instincts and affections' (which are taken from the marriage service in the 1928 Prayer Book) are the Canon's gloss on the second cause of matrimony in the *Book of Common Prayer*. The point made by this gloss is that it is marriage that allows natural human instincts and affections (including the natural human desire for a sexual relationship) to find expression in a way that is holy and that is in accord with the way that God has created his human creatures to live. The Canon expresses this point in a positive way, but by corollary it also supports the point made explicitly in the *Book of Common Prayer* and the *Homilies* that the expression of human desires and instincts outside of marriage is unholy, and not in accordance with God's will. We know that the Canon needs to be read in this way for two reasons.

(i) the Canon itself states explicitly that 'The teaching of our Lord affirmed by the Church of England is expressed and maintained in the Form of solemnisation of Matrimony contained in the Book of Common Prayer.' This means that the Church of England still upholds the Prayer Book description of extra-marital sex as 'fornication' and it is illegitimate to read the wording of Canon B.30 in a way that contradicts this fact.

(ii) In addition, we know that when the words about the 'hallowing and right direction of the natural instincts and affections' were included in the 1928 Prayer Book and then in Canon B.30, the position of the Church of England was unequivocally that sex outside marriage was sin. It is therefore unhistorical to read the words as if they are intended to provide Canonical support for the possibility of sex outside marriage.

Hamley is likewise misleading in what she writes about the preface to the *Common Worship* marriage service. There is no evidence that those who wrote this preface, or the preface to the Alternative Service

Book marriage service on which it is based, were
seeking to reflect a changed understanding of the
importance of sexual intercourse being confined to
marriage. Had this been the purpose of the text, it
would never have been approved by the House of
Bishops or by General Synod. Hamley is reading into
the text something it was not intended to indicate.

The real motivating factor behind the wording in
the Common Worship preface was the desire to be
sensitive to the pastoral needs of those coming to be
married in church in the twenty-first century.

The omission of 'brute beasts,' 'carnal lusts' and
the idea of marriage as a remedy for sin and the
inclusion of references to a sexual relationship as a
positive part of marriage were an attempt to counter
the popular belief that the Christian faith takes a
negative view of sex.

In the sixteenth century it was important for the
Church of England to emphasise that marriage was
not just about sexual activity and the procreation of
children, but also about a 'friendly fellowship' of love
between husbands and wives and the bringing up of
children in the Christian faith. This is therefore what
is emphasised in the *Book of Common Prayer* and in
the homily 'Of the State of Matrimony.' At the start of
the twenty-first century, it was felt that what needed
to be underlined was that the Church of England
takes a positive view of sexual activity, hence the
wording in *Common Worship*.

It should also be noted that the material in
Common Worship is authorised because it is judged

to be in line with the doctrine contained in the Prayer Book and the other historic formularies of the Church of England.[49] The hermeneutical principle that follows from this is that the Common Worship material needs to be read in a way that is in line with the teaching of the Prayer Book and the other historic formularies. This means that even apart from the historical issue just mentioned, it is an illegitimate move to contrast what is said in the marriage services in the Prayer Book and in *Common Worship*. The continuing doctrinal authority of the Prayer Book means that the two need to be read in a complementary, rather than a contrasting, fashion.

Finally, Hamley is also misleading when at the end of her paper she constantly distinguishes between 'Holy Matrimony' and 'civil marriage.' What she fails to recognise is that in the Prayer Book and Canon B.30 'Holy Matrimony' is simply a synonym for 'marriage.' For the Church of England, marriage is the way of life instituted by God at creation and defined in Canon B.30. Opposite-sex marriages conducted by clergy in church, and those conducted by registrars in a registry office or some other civil setting (which is what 'civil marriage' means), are both valid forms of marriage because they both conform to the form of marriage instituted by God. The problem with same-sex civil marriages is not that they are civil ceremonies, but that, being contrary to the nature of marriage as instituted by God, they are not marriages at all.

---

49. Canon B2.1

It follows that the answer to Hamley's question of why a church that refuses to perform same-sex marriages would nevertheless dedicate or bless civil marriages, is simple. Civil marriages are marriages, and can therefore be rightly dedicated to God and blessed in his name. From the traditional Christian viewpoint, same-sex marriages are not really marriages at all, but a humanly created alternative to marriage. As such they can be neither dedicated to God nor blessed in his name. To do so would arguably be a breach of the third commandment in that it would involve taking the name of God in vain.

PART III

A biblical theology of blessing, and why it rules out the blessing of same-sex relationships

From a biblical perspective, God's blessing of humanity is the action that God takes to enable human beings to flourish in the way he has intended for them from before the creation of the world. God freely decides to create, he decides how he wants his human creatures to flourish, and he blesses them by putting in place the conditions for this to happen.

The biblical pattern of blessing

If we look at the biblical narrative as a whole, we can discern a recurring but developing pattern in the conditions which God puts in place to enable human beings to flourish. As the Australian biblical scholar Graeme Goldsworthy has noted, what God repeatedly puts in place is the ability of human beings to live as God's people, in the place given to them by God and under God's kingly rule as mediated by his word.[50]

Following Goldsworthy, we can set out this threefold pattern of blessing as it is developed through Scripture:

---

50. Graeme Goldsworthy, *Gospel and Kingdom* (Carlisle: The Paternoster Press, 1994), p51

	GOD'S PEOPLE	GOD'S PLACE	GOD'S RULE
Eden	Adam and Eve	The Garden	God's word
Israel	Abraham	Canaan	Abrahamic Covenant
	Israel under Moses	Promised land	Sinai Covenant
	Israel under monarchy	Land, Jerusalem temple	Sinai Covenant
Prophecy	Faithful remnant	Restored land, Jerusalem temple	New covenant written on the heart
New Testament	New Israel – those 'in Christ' both Jews and Gentiles	New temple – God's people where Christ dwells	New covenant, the rule of Christ through the Spirit

The final fulfilment of this pattern, and the completion of God's purposes of blessing, is the new creation described in Revelation 21-22 where people from all nations dwell in the immediate presence of God in the New Jerusalem which is also Eden restored.

There are three key things to note about this biblical pattern of blessing.

First, the new covenant promised by the prophets and brought in by Christ is the fulfilment rather than the abrogation of the Sinai covenant. If we look carefully at the New Testament, we find that it teaches that the law given on Sinai is still in force, although its application has changed in some respects under the new dispensation (thus circumcision and the offering of the sacrifices laid down in Leviticus are no longer required).

Secondly in every stage, trust and obedience are required for people to enjoy God's blessing. People have to trust that what God says is for their good, and obey accordingly. To put it in New Testament terms, what is constantly required is the 'obedience of faith' (Romans 1:5, 16:26), that is to say the obedience to God that is produced or caused by faith. Faith is trust in God's purposes of blessing, and obedience flows from this.

Thirdly, when people fail to trust and obey, they forfeit the blessing that God wants to give them. Adam and Eve eat the forbidden fruit and are expelled from the Garden of Eden, the people of Israel turn from God to idols and break his law, and are exiled from the land of promise, and at the last judgement 'those who do not obey the gospel of our Lord Jesus' suffer 'the punishment of eternal destruction and exclusion from the presence of the Lord and from the glory of his might' (1 Thessalonians 1:8-9).

Blessing, marriage and sexual conduct

If we go back to the account in Genesis of the initial form of blessing bestowed on Adam and Eve, we find that a central part of this blessing is God bringing them together in sexual union (Genesis 2:18-45) which eventually becomes the context in which they fulfil God's injunction to 'be fruitful and multiply' (Genesis

2:28, 4:1 and 4:25). This aspect of their blessing is also depicted as having permanent significance.

The comment by the narrator in Genesis 2:24: 'Therefore a man leaves his father and his mother and cleaves to his wife, and they become one flesh' indicates that God's bringing together of the first man and woman is the origin of the social institution of marriage. Human beings in subsequent generations come together in the same way as the first couple in the garden did. Furthermore, as Robert Lawton observes, the word translated 'leaves' in the RSV actually means 'shall leave'. Consequently, the verse expresses 'a description of divine intention rather than a habitually observed fact'.[51] Genesis 2:24 is saying that God ordained marriage as the continuing expression of his blessing of human beings as male and female.

As we move on from Eden through the rest of the Old Testament we find that an integral part of living rightly before God in trustful obedience is fidelity to the marital pattern set out in Genesis 2:24. Whenever forms of marriage or sexual conduct contrary to this pattern are referred to in the Old Testament, they are explicitly or implicitly viewed as contrary to the will of God.

For example, in Leviticus 18: 4-5 the people of Israel under the Mosaic dispensation are warned: 'You shall do my ordinances and keep my statutes

---

51. Robert B Lawton, 'Genesis 2:24: Trite or Tragic?', *The Journal of Biblical Literature*, 105, 1986, p98

and walk in them. I am the Lord your God. You shall therefore keep my statutes and ordinances, by doing which a man shall live: I am the Lord.' If we ask what it means to keep the Lord's statues and ordinances the answer given by the rest of the chapter is that it involves eschewing all forms of sexual activity outside heterosexual marriage.

As John Richardson notes, in the New Testament, Old Testament sexual ethics are still regarded as binding on those who wish to enjoy the blessing of God under the new covenant. In his words:

> Even more so than under the Old Covenant, heterosexual marriage is consistently presented under the New Covenant as the proper context for sexual activity, outside of which there is only adultery and fornication.[52]

For example, in 1 Thessalonians 4:1-8 Paul describes what it means to live a life in obedience to God as follows:

> Finally, brethren, we beseech and exhort you in the Lord Jesus, that as you learned from us how you ought to live and to please God, just as you are doing, you do so more and more. For you know what instructions we gave you through the Lord Jesus. For this is the will of God, your sanctification: that you abstain from unchastity; that each one of you know how to take a wife for himself in holiness and honour, not in the passion of lust like heathen who do not know God; that no man transgress, and wrong his brother in this matter,

---

52. John Richardson, *What God has made clean...* (Epsom, The Good Book Company, 2003), Kindle ed, Loc 590.

because the Lord is an avenger in all these things, as we solemnly forewarned you. For God has not called us for uncleanness, but in holiness. Therefore whoever disregards this, disregards not man but God, who gives his Holy Spirit to you.

The word translated 'unchastity' in the RSV is the Greek word *porneia*, a catch-all term for all forms of sexual activity outside marriage. Paul's teaching is clear. If you want to engage in sexual activity then you have to be married and restrict your sexual activity to that context.

In similar fashion, the writer to the Hebrews declares: 'Let marriage be held in honour among all, and let the marriage bed be kept undefiled; for God will judge the immoral and adulterous.' (Hebrews 13:4) As the Church of England Evangelical Council report, *Guarding the Deposit*, explains:

> The sexual ethic that is taught in these and other passages is one that is rooted in the teaching of Genesis 1 and 2 about God's creation of human beings as men and women and about marriage as the setting for sexual union between a man and a woman leading to procreation; and in the observable fact that the bodies of men and women are designed for heterosexual sexual intercourse leading to reproduction (this is a key part of St Paul's argument in Romans 1).
>
> According to the apostles, therefore, Christian believers should practise sexual fidelity within marriage and sexual abstinence outside it, and marriage should

be marked by a relationship that is patterned on the relationship between Christ and the Church. (Ephesians 5:21-33, 1 Corinthians 7:1-4)

Because this is the teaching of the apostles, this sexual ethic has been followed ever since by orthodox Christians. C S Lewis thus speaks for the whole of the Christian tradition when he writes in *Mere Christianity*: 'There is no getting away from it; the Christian rule is, 'Either marriage, with complete faithfulness to your partner, or else total abstinence.'[53]

It also needs to be noted that the New Testament is quite clear that if people fail to trust and obey God by observing this ethic, and do not repent, then they face the prospect of forfeiting God's blessing at the last judgement. That is what Paul means when he writes that 'the Lord in an avenger in these things' and what the writer to the Hebrews means when he warns that 'God will judge the immoral and the adulterous.'

Part of the rejection of all sexual activity outside marriage by the New Testament is a rejection of gay and lesbian sexual activity, a point which, contrary to the claims made by Moberly and in the LLF book, is quite clear.

To quote *Guarding the Deposit* again:

---

53. The Church of England Evangelical Council, *Guarding the Deposit*, p2 at https://ceec.info/wp-content/uploads/2022/10/guarding_the_deposit.pdf First published 2016. This edition 2022

50

Various forms of same-sex sexual relationships, both between men and men and between women and women—including long-lasting consensual relationships and even same-sex marriages—existed in the first-century Greco-Roman world, and would have been known about by the early Christians. Theirs was a world with just as much sexual variety as exists today.

However, the apostolic teaching recorded in the New Testament makes no concession to this variety. There is instead a conscious and deliberate rejection of it. Following the teaching of Jesus himself (Mark7:21), it views same-sex relationships as a form of porneia — that is, a form of immoral sexual activity forbidden by God's law given to Israel in the book of Leviticus.

For the writers of the New Testament same-sex relationships are:

- a manifestation of the disorder in human relationships caused by humanity's turning away from its creator (Romans 1:26-27);
- a form of behaviour, contrary to God's law (1 Corinthians 6:9-11); a form of behaviour that is contrary to the 'gospel' and 'sound doctrine' (1Timothy 1:10);
- an example of the sort of sexual immorality that will attract the eternal judgement of God (Jude 7);
- a form of behaviour excluding one from God's kingdom, but from which Christians can be set free by the work of Jesus and the Spirit (1 Corinthians 6:9-11).

Richard Hays notes in his study *The Moral Vision of the New Testament*:

> ...the New Testament offers no loopholes or exception clauses that might allow for the acceptance of homosexual practice under some circumstances. Despite the efforts of some recent interpreters to explain away the evidence, the New Testament remains unambiguous and univocal in its condemnation of homosexual conduct.'[54]

Although there is no specific discussion of same-sex marriage in the New Testament, there can be absolutely no doubt what the New Testament writers would have thought of the idea. They would have regarded it as doubly immoral not only because it involved same-sex sexual activity, but also because it was a parody of the form of marriage which God himself had instituted at creation (see Matthew 19:4-5).

A final point that needs to recognised is that the biblical witness about homosexual conduct has been universally accepted by orthodox Christians until very recent times. As Donald Fortson and Rollin Grams put it, 'the historic understanding held by Christians for two millennia' has been that 'homosexual practice is incompatible with Christian discipleship, and church discipline may be necessary if the practice is habitual.'[55]

---

54. Richard Hays, *The Moral Vision of the New Testament* (Edinburgh: T&T Clark, 2001), p394
55. *Guarding the Deposit*, pp2-3

CONCLUSION

God's sovereignty and consistency, and the proposal to bless same-sex relationships

Moberly and Hamley have failed to make a legitimate case for the Church of England to bless same-sex sexual relationships. Indeed it is also clear that it would be impossible for anyone to do this.

The reason for that is because God is sovereign in blessing. According to Scripture it is God who decides to bless, and decides what blessing shall involve. Human beings do not get a say in the matter. They cannot determine who or what God will and will not bless.

As David Stubbs notes in his commentary on Numbers, this truth is highlighted in the story of Balak and Balaam in Numbers 22-24. Here we are told how Balak, king of Moab, hires the seer Balaam to curse the people of Israel, but Balaam repeatedly blesses them instead. To quote Stubbs:

> Propositioned by Balak to curse Israel, Balaam in his activity as a seer comes into contact with YHWH the God of Israel. His interactions with YHWH challenge the assumptions of his typical magico-religious practices. The person of Balaam embodies the clash between two

very different ways of envisioning and responding to God and gods.

The lesson of the text is clear: as opposed to the assumptions of typical magico-religious practises in the surrounding cultures, YHWH is not simply another God or spirit whose power can be used by magicians and kings to bring blessing and cursing as they see fit. The worldview represented by Balak is ultimately shown to be false. Balak's unsuccessful attempt to control Balaam, and Balaam's unsuccessful attempt to control his donkey, parody their lack of control over forces that are larger than they realise. Instead of Balak using God through Balaam to curse Israel, it is God who uses kings and prophets and magicians to bring forward God's purposes of blessing. Many of the confessions and statements that Balaam makes also reflect this understanding by upholding the transcendence and freedom of God in light of human activity. In contrast to Balak's statement in 22:6, Balaam says that he is subject to 'the word of the LORD' (24:13) and only in accordance with the will of God can he speak blessings or curses upon Israel. He counters Balak's pretensions with statements that point to the ineffectiveness of these magical practises, turns his back on the rights of divination (24:1; cf 23:23), and confesses that his will cannot bring forth blessing or curse on its own (24:13).

While these chapters might be interpreted as merely pointing to YHWH being more powerful than the spiritual forces assumed in the world of Balak, we also see Balaam coming to a deeper understanding. God's relationship to Israel is of a different quality altogether, the kind of relationship between gods and people that Balak and Balaam himself had presupposed. God cannot be controlled or manipulated. In fact, God transcends the battle of creaturely forces. In relation to such a God, the only proper role someone like Balaam can play is that of *mediating* God's power, the proper role of the Israelite priest and prophet, as opposed to *manipulating* God's power, the role often assumed by the seer or sorcerer.[56]

God's freedom in blessing, highlighted in this story in Numbers, means that the role of the Church in blessing is to mediate God's power by making its words of prayer the channel by which God blesses what he wishes to bless.

Prayers of blessing in the marriage service

Seen from this perspective the prayers of blessing at the end of the marriage service in the *Book of Common Prayer* are entirely proper. These prayers recall God's acts of blessing in Scripture, and ask that God will continue this revealed pattern of blessing in the lives of the two people who have just been married.

> O God of Abraham, God of Isaac, God of Jacob, bless these thy servants, and sow the seed of eternal life in their hearts; that whatsoever in thy holy Word they shall profitably learn, they may in deed fulfil the same. Look, O Lord, mercifully upon them from heaven, and bless

56. David Stubbs, *Numbers* (London: SCM, 2009), pp180-181

them. And as thou didst send thy blessing upon Abraham and Sarah, to their great comfort, so vouchsafe to send thy blessing upon these thy servants; that they obeying thy will, and alway being in safety under thy protection, may abide in thy love unto their lives' end; through Jesus Christ our Lord. Amen.

[This Prayer next following shall be omitted, where the Woman is past child-bearing.]

O merciful Lord, and heavenly Father, by whose gracious gift mankind is increased: We beseech thee, assist with thy blessing these two persons, that they may both be fruitful in procreation of children, and also live together so long in godly love and honesty, that they may see their children Christianly and virtuously brought up, to thy praise and honour; through Jesus Christ our Lord. Amen.

O God, who by thy mighty power hast made all things of nothing; who also (after other things set in order) didst appoint, that out of man (created after thine own image and similitude) woman should take her beginning; and, knitting them together, didst teach that it should never be lawful to put asunder those whom thou by Matrimony hadst made one: O God, who hast consecrated the state of Matrimony to such an excellent mystery, that in it is signified and represented the spiritual marriage and unity betwixt Christ and his Church: Look mercifully upon these thy servants, that both this man may love his wife, according to thy Word, (as Christ did love his spouse the Church, who gave himself for it, loving and cherishing it even as his own flesh,) and also that this woman may be loving and amiable, faithful and obedient to her husband; and in all quietness, sobriety, and peace, be a follower of holy and godly matrons. O Lord, bless them both, and grant them to inherit thy everlasting kingdom; through Jesus Christ our Lord. Amen.

Then shall the Priest say,

Almighty God, who at the beginning did create our first parents, Adam and Eve, and did sanctify and join them together in marriage; Pour upon you the riches of his grace, sanctify and bless you, that ye may please him both in body and soul, and live together in holy love unto your lives' end. Amen.

Underlying these prayers are two fundamental Christian beliefs. God is sovereign and God is consistent. Because God is sovereign, he decides the nature of blessing, but because God is consistent, we can expect him to act now in line with how he has acted in the past. What God has blessed; we can expect him to continue to bless.

By contrast with these prayers from the Prayer Book marriage service, prayers for the blessing of same-sex sexual relationships go against belief in God's sovereignty and consistency.[57]

---

57. Whether the language used is that of blessing same-sex sexual relationships, or praying for the blessing of such relationships, or seeking for God's blessing in relation to such relationships, the point remains the same. Prayer is being offered that God will act to bless the relationship concerned.

In effect, even if not in intention, such prayers go against God's sovereignty because they assume that we can rightly ask God to bless forms of relationship that according to Scripture he has never decided to bless. According to Scripture, God has decided to bless marriage between a man and a woman, and sexual activity in that context. What is now being proposed is that we can also ask God to bless same-sex sexual relationships and marriages as well, even though there is nothing at all in Scripture that says he wishes to do so. This means that either the prayers are pointless, or we think we can go back to the magico-religious approach rejected in Numbers and make God bless what we want him to bless.

Such prayers also go against God's consistency. As we have seen, Scripture makes clear that same-sex sexual activity (and by extension same-sex marriage) are forms of sin which are inconsistent with the trusting obedience to God necessary to receive God's blessing. In effect, even if not in intention, prayers for the blessing of same-sex sexual relationships involve saying that we no longer have to take what God says about the matter in Scripture as binding. God has (apparently) changed his mind and is now happy to bless such relationships. Why else would we pray for him to do so? However: 'God is not man, that he should lie, or a son of man, that he should repent. Has he said, and will he not do it? Or has he spoken, and will he not fulfil it?' (Numbers 23:19).

IN SUMMARY

In Scripture God reveals that he wills to bless his human creatures, and the basic pattern of such blessing has remained consistent in this world and will remain consistent in the world to come. God blesses his people as they live in the place that he has given to them, and as they live in trusting obedience under his kingly rule. Thus it has been, thus it is now, and thus it shall be forever.

Part of living in trusting obedience is accepting God's decision that men and women should join together in marriage and have sex only in that context. Deciding not to accept that decision or not to live according to it is sin and leads to people forfeiting the blessing God wants to give them.

It can never be right to introduce prayers for the blessing of same-sex sexual relationships and same-sex marriages, because to do so would implicitly reject God's sovereignty and consistency. It would involve the implicit claim that we can manipulate God.

The *Prayers of Love and Faith* proposals mean that we stand at a critical moment in the history of the Church of England. We will have to decide whether we will allow God to be God, or whether we will instead go our own way, invoking the name of God in support of things which are contrary to his will. As we face this choice let us turn to God in prayer asking that he will give us the grace to make the right decision.

'O Lord, we beseech thee mercifully to receive the prayers of thy people which call upon thee, and grant that they may both perceive and know what things they ought to do, and also may have grace and power faithfully to do the same; through Jesus Christ our Lord. Amen

(The collect for the First Sunday after Epiphany in the *Book of Common Prayer*)

Dr Martin Davie is a theological consultant to the Church of England Evangelical Council (CEEC). From 2000-2013 he was the Theological Secretary to the Church of England's Council for Christian Unity, Theological Consultant to the House of Bishops, and Secretary of the Faith and Order Commission

'Clarity and brevity are two great gifts to the world.'

Dictum's books do not waste words, or waste the reader's time. They bring biblical thinking which is refreshing, clear and well-applied.

Dictum has four lists:

Dictum Essentials: Core books for wide use in churches and mission agencies, with questions for personal reflection or discussion.

Oxbridge: Church history from the ancient university towns of Oxford and Cambridge. Including a Reformation Walking Tour; and a humorous feline view of Oxford.

Unique angles on John Stott's ministry, including the remarkable story of Frances Whitehead, his secretary for 55 years, a story which needs to be preserved; and a fun authorized children's biography.

List Four: A growing and diverse wider list of pithy books, longer and shorter.

dictumpress.com
books worth reading more than once